49 Excuses for Extending Your Summer Holiday

Copyright © 2019, 2022 by James Warwood

Published by Curious Squirrel Press

All rights reserved

No part of this book may be used, stored or reproduced in any manner whatsoever without written permission from the author or publisher.

Book cover design by: James Warwood
Book interior design by: Mala Letra / Lic. Sara F. Salomon

ISBN: 9781915646262
ebook ISBN: B07T4JSYGQ

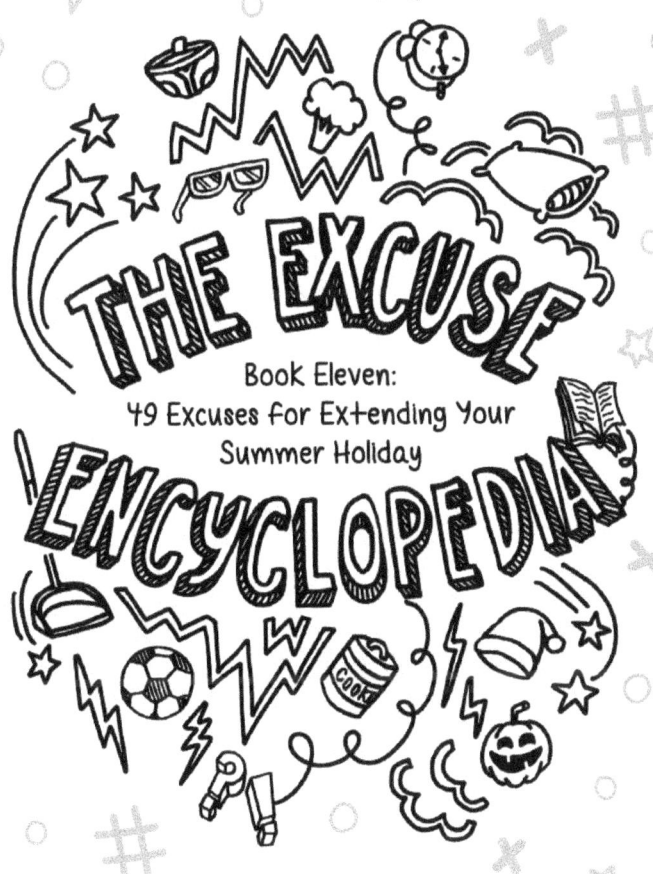

THE EXCUSE ENCYCLOPEDIA

Book Eleven:
49 Excuses for Extending Your Summer Holiday

James Warwood

BOOK ELEVEN

Home-Schooling is the Future

HOLIDAY EXCUSES

1. THE TREE-SCHOOL EXCUSE

Have you heard the news? A new school has opened at the bottom of the garden . . .

. . . Our old treehouse has been converted into a brand-new school especially for me. The curriculum is cartoons and the lunch break is *8* hours long. And the best bit is that no other children are allowed in and absolutely no teachers either.

2. THE SELF-TEACHER EXCUSE

I know what you are thinking. How can a child also be a teacher? . . .

. . . Let me answer that question with another question. Are there any teachers in the history of the Education System who have NOT consulted the *All-Knowing-Teacher.* I'm simply cutting out the middle-man. Go on. Ask me the hardest question you can think of and I'll reply with the correct answer.

3. THE TV EDUCATION EXCUSE

Let me introduce you to my new teacher...

...I call her Teacher-Vision. In the morning she shows me the current affairs (the News Channel), then she teaches me important daytime knowledge (Daytime TV Shows), and then in the afternoon, she introduces me to economy and advanced maths (the Shopping Channels).

4. THE CLEVER EXCUSE

Now that I've learnt everything I can from big school my superior intellect is needed at home...

... So, grab a pen and paper, take a seat and start learning from my amazing mind.

5. THE TEACHER OF HOMES EXCUSE

I've mastered the art of Home Schooling . . .

. . . These rebellious and ninny nincompoop numbskull homes all need a good teacher. So, I've decided to don the tweed and inspire them to grow up to become successful and happy homes. It's going to be my life's work.

BOOK ELEVEN

New Business Ventures

6. THE TAKE AWAY EXCUSE

I've been doing some thinking. School kids get to go on all sorts of amazing trips...

... So I've set up a company called *Teacher Away Days*. So far I've got planned a trip to the Pencil Factory, the hill where some old bloke in history said 'charge' and then ate a sandwich, and the centre of an active volcano. The very first trip is on the first day of school. How would you like to go on a two-week expedition to the moon?

7. THE SUPPLY TEACHER EXCUSE

The animals at the zoo always look bored and the Supply Teachers at school always look overworked . . .

. . . So, I've created a business that encourages a job swap with local schools and local zoos. A hyena could teach Geography Teacher because the subject is a joke. A parrot could teacher French Teacher because it can speak fluent gibberish. And a monkey be a headteacher because if you're naughty in class you would get something even worse than a detention thrown at your face.

8. THE ONLINE PUPILS EXCUSE

See you later, I'm going to school . .

. . . Let me introduce you to my summer holiday invention – the Remote Controlled iStudent. While I stay at home in my warm bed this wonderful machine will go to school for me. Thanks to the web camera and microphone I can fully participate in every single lesson. Plus, if this thing works, I'm going to be a millionaire.

9. THE WORK EXPERIENCE EXCUSE

I'd love to come back to school, but first I have to complete my work experience...

... First, I'm at the Car Wash for six weeks, then the Supermarket for six weeks, then the Bank for six weeks, and then the Chocolate Factory for the rest of my life. So, if you stay in my good books, I'll wash your car, get you a discount on your groceries, re-mortgage your house and supply you with free chocolate for life. Do we have a deal?

10. THE HAMSTER HEADTEACHER EXCUSE

While everyone was off school for the summer holidays the Headmaster was sacked and replaced by a hamster...

...The Hamster Headmaster is our new dictator. It makes the school rules now and it told everyone to go home and go back to bed. The teachers are right, budget cuts are the best!

BOOK ELEVEN

Got a New Job

11. THE ADULT MINDER EXCUSE

I can't go back to school because kids aren't my target audience for my new public service...

...Do you have an adult who needs supervising? Then contact 'The Adult Minders' the new service that provides award-winning adult care run by fully qualified responsible children. I can't wait to give them to him. He's gonna love 'em!

12. ICE CREAM TASTER EXCUSE

I can no longer devote my time to education . . .

. . . I have an extremely important full-time job that requires my full attention. I taste and review ice cream for a living. I know what you're thinking, it's a tough job but someone has got to do it.

13. THE INJURY LAWYER EXCUSE

Did you have an accident while on your summer holiday that wasn't your fault? . . .

. . . Then call me and I'll help you get an extra month off school without any homework.

14. THE SCHOOL CARETAKER EXCUSE

Right, I'm off to work as the new School Caretaker . . .

. . . I've already changed the lock on the staff room door, persuaded the dinner ladies to spit in the headteachers coffee and swapped the toilet paper in the students' toilets for triple-ply with a hint of tea tree. Now then, off I go to open a second-hand jumble sale in the playground to sell off all the lost property so that I can buy a flat-screen TV for the caretaker's room.

15. THE SECRET AGENT EXCUSE

Bye, I'm off to school now . . .

. . . *[whisper]* but I'm secretly working for the government as a secret agent to uncover a conspiracy that could cripple the National Education System, but I'm actually at the centre of that same conspiracy working against the government as a mole so that we bring down the National Education System from within.

BOOK ELEVEN

Major Change in the Education System

HOLIDAY EXCUSES

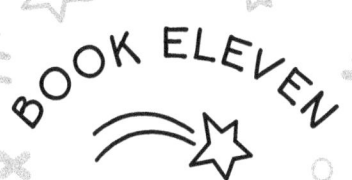

16. THE NEW WORLD ORDER EXCUSE

Haven't you heard the news? The whole world has been invaded and conquered by massive alien robot pigeons . . .

. . . Everyone has to stop going to school or work and instead go outside and play in the park, drop chips on the floor and comb our new overlords metallic feathers. It's what the alien robot pigeons want.

17. VICTORIAN REGRESSION EXCUSE

Haven't you heard the news? The government has reverted all our laws back to the Victorian Era . . .

. . . All children over the age of five have to go to work in factories, shine shoes or sweep chimneys. I choose the last one because I thought I'd get to tap dance across the rooftops of London like they do in Mary Poppins, but I was wrong.

18. THE VIKING INVASION EXCUSE

Haven't you heard the news? The Vikings have invaded, again . . .

. . . At first, they only came back because they had left their phone chargers, but now that we've got good 5G coverage they've decided to stick around and rule over us with tyranny, cruelty and constant Facebook messages about the latest Ikea catalogue.

19. THE SCHOOL OF LIFE EXCUSE

Haven't you heard the news? All schools have been shut down by the government and children are to follow in their parent's footsteps instead...

... You caught me practising with your shoes. So, I've got to come to work with you and learn your trade. Let's go to work. (Note: this will only work if your parents are not School Teachers, Classroom Assistants or a Dinnerlady).

20. THE SCHOOL INSPECTORS EXCUSE

Haven't you heard the news? The School Inspectors closed the school due to poor standards . . .

. . . I have to wait in my pyjamas until another letter arrives from the Education Board to tell me which school I have to go to instead. Let's hope the postal service is as slow and unreliable as it always has been.

BOOK ELEVEN

Unexpected Delay to Your Holiday Abroad

HOLIDAY EXCUSES

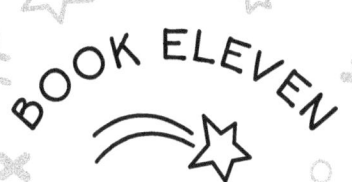

21. THE NEGOTIATOR EXCUSE

Here's the deal, Miss Print. I'll not come back to school . . .

. . . That's right. I'll make your life so much easier by not being in your classroom and all you need to do is tick my name on the register every day. But be warned, if you don't take my deal I'll ask 5 extremely awkward questions a day, here are a few to wet your appetite (for inspiration see *49 Questions to Annoy Your Parents*).

22. THE SCHOOL IN BERMUDA EXCUSE

Dear Teacher. With regret, I write to you from Bermuda to inform you I am not coming back to school . . .

. . . After going to the Caribbean for my summer holiday I decided to attend the local school, who have offered me a job. I am Professor of Sunbathing and Afternoon Naps. It was an offer I couldn't refuse. See you in a year!

23. THE TIME-ZONE EXCUSE

What are you talking about. Summer hasn't just finished, it's just begun . . .

. . . I've decided to change time zones to Australia's, which means while you're all just finishing your summer holiday I'm about to start mine. I'm off to go and throw another shrimp on the BBQ. See you all in six weeks.

24. THE GLOBAL WARMING EXCUSE

Bad news everyone. Global Warming is here which means it's going to always be summertime . . .

. . . Which means autumn will never arrive. Which means it will always the summer holiday. Which means it will never be the start of school ever again. My advice, move to the beach and start stockpiling sun cream.

25. THE EXTENSION LETTER EXCUSE

Didn't you hear? I applied for a summer holiday extension . . .

BEST LETTER EVER!

. . . It was accepted, of course. What is the extension for? I didn't manage to sleep in past 1 pm, finish reading the Harry Potter series (both the books and the films) or master a new dance move. See you in two weeks.

BOOK ELEVEN

Too Clever for School

26. THE UNI EXCUSE

Hi and bye . . .

. . . I know this is the first day back after the summer holidays but I just came to say goodbye. I'm so brainy I've been given a scholarship to Oxford University seven years earlier. I'll be Prime Minister in no time, at which point I'm going to make my first policy change to double the school summer holidays.

27. THE SPECIAL CLASSROOM EXCUSE

See ya, I'm off to McDonald's . . .

. . . Didn't you know? My old school tragically burnt down over the summer holidays. Thankfully the kind and generous fast-food chain offered their restaurant as our temporary classroom. Now I can have fries with my maths work.

28. THE BITTEN EXCUSE

I was bitten by the ghost of Albert Einstein and now I'm super intelligent . . .

. . . In fact, I'm now so clever that I can now predict the future. You're going to agree with me that it's pointless I go back school and then we're both going to eat chocolate and watch TV.

29. THE NEW SYLLABUS EXCUSE

As I am the smartest kid in school I was asked to rewrite the school syllabus . . .

. . . And here it is – the new and improved Silly Bus. All aboard, next stop is another six week holiday at the beach.

30. THE TEACHER SCHOOL EXCUSE

Welcome to your first day at Teacher School...

... The world has finally realised that age has nothing to do with intelligence and so have decided to make certain adults go back to school. As I'm so brainy I've been appointed as your new teacher. Finish class is Dodgeball. We're going to have so much fun.

BOOK ELEVEN

Struck Down by an Illness

31. THE MADE-UP EXCUSE

Don't look this up in the dictionary, but I have Tyrani-nanni-hyper-biscuit-itus . . .

. . . It's a terrible illness where I think I'm an angry old person who only eats biscuits. Please may I be excused so I can go back to the old peoples home and shout at the TV until I fall asleep?

32. ALLERGIC TO TEACHERS EXCUSE

The doctors have discovered why I hate school so much. It's because I'm allergic to teachers . . .

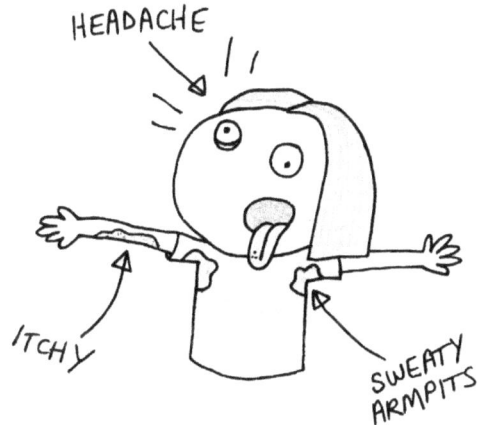

. . . When you think about it, it all makes sense. Whenever I'm in a classroom I get itchy. When the teacher asks me a question I get a headache. And when I hear the word *homework* I get hot and sweaty and my vision goes blurry and I start to blackout. Maybe I should go lay down at least a mile away from any teachers.

33. THE ANTI-INSOMNIAC EXCUSE

You know how I'm always falling asleep in your classes . . .

. . . Well, turns out it's not because of your teaching style, it's because I'm an Anti-Insomniac. That means I'm tired ALL the time. I've been ordered by the doctor to spend all year in bed so I just came into school to say see you all next academic year. Night night.

34. THE UNCOMMON-COLD EXCUSE

Don't come near me. I've caught an uncommon cold . . .

. . . It's exactly the same as a common cold except for one small difference. You get 100% more snot. There aren't enough tissues in the world to stop these two green rivers. Evacuate the classroom for your own safety. Anyone who can't swim, it was nice knowing you.

35. THE D & V & E.L.F EXCUSE

I can't come back to school as I've been signed off by the doctor with D & V & E.L.F . . .

. . . Never heard of it? Its full name is diarrhoea and vomiting and extremely lethal flatulence. Uh oh. If everyone doesn't clear out of this classroom in the next 10 seconds you'll also get a demonstration.

BOOK ELEVEN

Holiday Drama That Won't Let Up

HOLIDAY EXCUSES

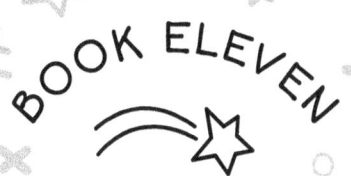

36. THE SKIING ACCIDENT EXCUSE

Is it possible to break every bone in your body? . . .

. . . I almost managed it. I skied into a tree and broke 203 out of 206 bones. I'll have to do my school work from the hospital by blinking at a computer screen. Thank God I didn't break my eyelids!

37. THE LOST MY PASSPORT EXCUSE

You know how people say never lose your passport while on holiday? . . .

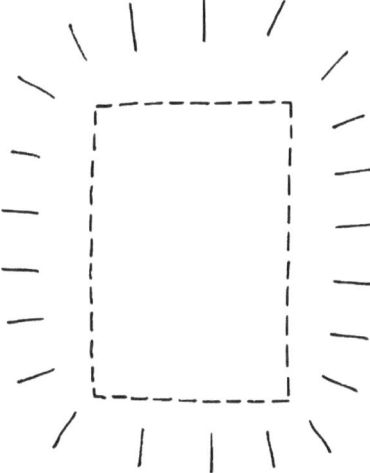

. . . I've found out why. It's because if you do lose your passport in a foreign country you're stuck there until you find it again. So, I'll try to make it back before Christmas but I've got the whole of Disneyland to search for my passport, including all of the rides and attractions.

38. THE ADOPTED BY LIONS EXCUSE

Whilst on Safari in Africa I learnt that Lions are very loving parents . . .

. . . After they ate my mum, dad and older sister they were full and so adopted me as one of their own. That's right, I'm a lion cub now. I think it would be best to let me skip the first few months of school and I'll persuade my new parents not to maul you to death at the next parents evening.

39. THE FELL DOWN A WELL EXCUSE

My name is Timmy and I fell down a well . . .

. . . Unfortunately, the Fire Brigade is on holiday, Lassie is having a manicure and my parents are enjoying the peace and quiet.

James Warwood

40. THE STILL QUEUING EXCUSE

I've finally reached the middle of the queue to go on Space Mountain! . . .

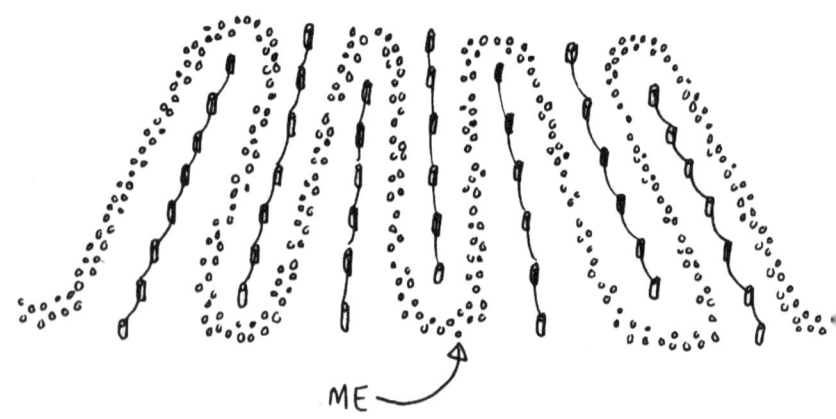

ME

. . . I can't go to school now. It would be a terrible waste of all this time if I leave the queue. I'll let you know if the rollercoaster was worth the three-week queue in one to two weeks time.

BOOK ELEVEN

Rich Kids Don't Need No Education

HOLIDAY EXCUSES

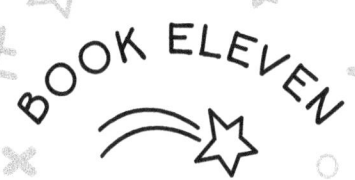

41. THE BOARDING SCHOOL EXCUSE

Now that my parents are filthy rich they're sending me to Boarding School...

... I am going to learn how to wear a sandwich board, how to write on whiteboards and how to shout 'All Aboard' like a Train Driver. No more English or Maths or stinky Geography for me.

42. THE SET FOR LIFE EXCUSE

The best thing about being filthy rich is that I'll never have to work a day in my life . . .

. . . So that means school is a waste of time for a rich kid like me. I think I'll go learn how to drive a speed boat instead of going to my French Lesson.

43. THE BOUGHT THE SCHOOL EXCUSE

Great news, Miss. My filthy rich parents bought the school over the summer holidays . . .

. . . They want all the teachers to reapply for their jobs and have appointed me to do the job interviews. Your gruelling interview will be in two weeks so you better go and get practising.

44. THE SUBSTITUTE PUPIL EXCUSE

Teachers are always getting Substitute Teachers when they can't teach...

... So I've been able to hire and pay for a Substitute Pupil. His name is Boris and he is the smartest kid in the world. He actually knows what all the buttons on a scientific calculator are for. I'm going to go for a nap while Boris takes this test for me.

45. THE MISSION TO MARS EXCUSE

I'm not coming back to school because I have become a Martian . . .

. . . I'm leaving Earth to become the first kid to live on Mars. Please, please tell me there's no school on Mars.

BOOK ELEVEN

Extremely Silly Excuses (that probably won't work)

HOLIDAY EXCUSES

46. THE SPECIAL BUTT EXCUSE

I've been saying it for years and now its official, my butt is special...

... Scientists from around the globe have all been applauding my behind and it's incredible powers. Apparently, my farts could be the key to beating world hunger, reversing climate change and curing cancer. If you need me I'll be in a secure top-secret laboratory trumping to save the planet.

47. THE PSYCHIC EXCUSE

I really would love to come back to school but what's the point when the world is going to end in five days . . .

. . . My psychic told me that there is an asteroid, an alien invasion and a deadly plague all heading for the earth that will destroy all humankind. On the bright side that gives me enough time to finish watching all my TV shows. Enjoy your last days of existence.

48. THE DATE DYSLEXIA EXCUSE

School started two weeks ago? Really!? . . .

. . . The doctor said this would happen. I've been told I have Date Dyslexia which means I can never work out which day of the year we are on. To be honest I thought it was either Christmas, Halloween or Dress Like a Unicorn Day. I feel like a complete idiot now.

49. THE COUNTDOWN EXCUSE

I'm here, I'm on time and I'm ready to learn . . .

. . . I understand that school is important for my future but, don't forget, holiday breaks are just as important for my mental health. So I've created this helpful countdown. 75 Schools Days to the Xmas Break. 139 School Days to the Spring Break. 199 Schools Day to next years Summer Holiday. Bring on the learning!

BONUS: LIBRARY CARD EXCUSE

I'm so excited for the first day back at school...

LIBRARY CARD

... Don't forget, you need to drop me off at the library now instead of school. That's where I'll be meeting my new one-to-one tutor (called YouTube).

BONUS: NEW SUPPLY TEACHER EXCUSE

Over the summer holidays I had an epiphany . . .

. . . The animals at the Zoo always look extremely bored and and the Supply Teachers at school always look extremely overworked. So, I've started a initiative that encourages job swaps between local schools and the nearby Zoo.

BONUS: GALACTIC APPRENTICESHIP EXCUSE

Good news, I don't have to go back to school . . .

. . . I got accepted onto an Apprenticeship Course. Apparently, my midi-chlorian count is very high which means I can go into a star ship and travel across the galaxy to the Jedi Temple on Coruscant.

BONUS: NO MORE EXAMS EXCUSE

The school exams have been updated . . .

. . . All of the exams are now 100% practical and require 0% revision time. So, that means no more studying all night and no more stupid lined paper or red-hot hand cramp from hours and hours of writing.

BONUS: PRIZE WINNINGS EXCUSE

Look Miss, I've been very busy over the summer holiday . . .

. . . I won the Nobel Prize, the Booker Prize and 1,352,759 Arcade Coupons. With all this prize money I'm set for life.

BONUS: INDEPENDENCE EXCUSE

I developed a condition over the summer holidays which means I can no longer attend school . . .

. . . It's called 'Independence'. I've realised I don't need to attend school to be a happy and successful human being. Now then, I'm going to go out into the world and make my fortune. Which way to Vegas?

BONUS: WARDROBE EXCUSE

Lucy, Edmond, Susan and Peter all thoroughly enjoyed their summer holiday in a wardrobe . . .

. . . But when I tried it I had an awful time. I am still lost. Please send a search party. And the worst part is I haven't found any Turkish Delight.

BONUS: CASH IN THE BAG EXCUSE

Teachers often complain about two things . . .

. . . 1. Having too much money, and 2. Having to deal with annoying kids, like me, who just keep on coming back. Well then, give me $1,000 and I can solve both of those problems.

BONUS: RUNNER FOR LIFE EXCUSE

Over the summer holiday I started running, and I've decided to never stop . . .

. . . You know, like Forrest Gump. So, until someone works out how to attach four wheels and an engine to my school I can't continue my education.

BONUS: PLASTIC NINJA EXCUSE

I can't come back to school because I've joined the fight against plastic pollution . . .

. . . I'm waging war on the non-biogradable, non-recyclable, ocean-destroying plastic polluting our world (and you should all join me).

BONUS: PILE OF UNATTENDED CASH EXCUSE

Oh look, a big pile of unattended cash...

... Now, if I was to go and take another six weeks holiday that would mean that you, my wonderful teacher, would be able to spend it on golden pencils, tea bags, potted plants and whatever else teachers like to spend money on.

James Warwood is a writer and illustrator who lives on the borders of North Wales with his wife, two sons, and cactus (called Steve the Cactus).

He has a degree in Theology, which at the time seemed like a great idea, until he released he didn't want to become an RE Teacher. Instead, he writes laugh-out-loud middle grade fiction and non-fiction. He also fills them with his silly cartoons. He is the bestselling author of the EXCUSE ENCYCLOPEDIA and the TRUTH OR POOP SERIES.

James likes whiskey, squirrels, reading silly books, playing his bass guitar, and Greggs Sausage Rolls. He does not like losing at board games or having to writing about himself in the third person.

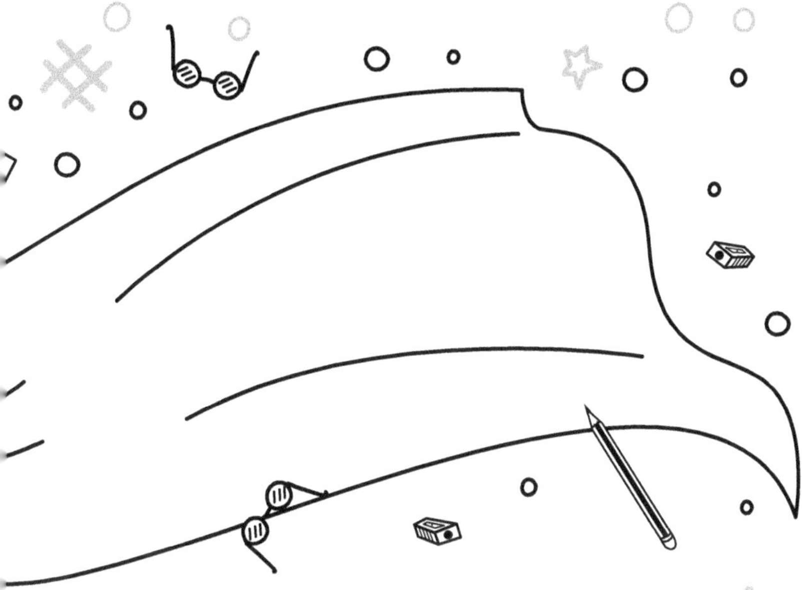

WHERE TO FIND JAMES ONLINE

Website: www.cjwarwood.com
Goodreads: James Warwood
Instagram: CJWarwood
Facebook: James Warwood

Want to join the
BOOKS & BISCUITS
CLUB?

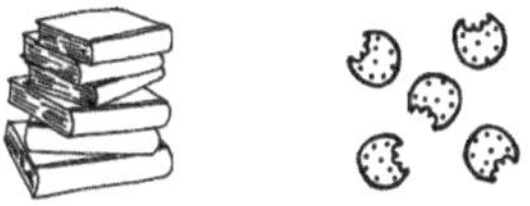

Scan me to sign up
to the newsletter.

  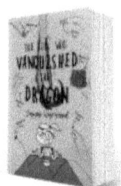

MIDDLE-GRADE STAND-ALONE FICTION

The Chef Who Cooked Up a Catastrophe
The Boy Who Stole One Million Socks
The Girl Who Vanquished the Dragon

TRUTH OR POOP SERIES

*True or false quiz books.
Learn something new and laugh as you do it!*

THE EXCUSE ENCYCLOPEDIA

11 more books to read!

GET THEM ALL IN THIS 12 IN 1 BUMPER EDITION!

820-page compendium of knowledge with 180 BONUS excuses

Scan me to activate your

25% DISCOUNT

www.ingramcontent.com/pod-product-compliance
Lightning Source LLC
Chambersburg PA
CBHW041314110526
44591CB00022B/2904